THIS EASTER COLORING BOOK BELONGS TO:

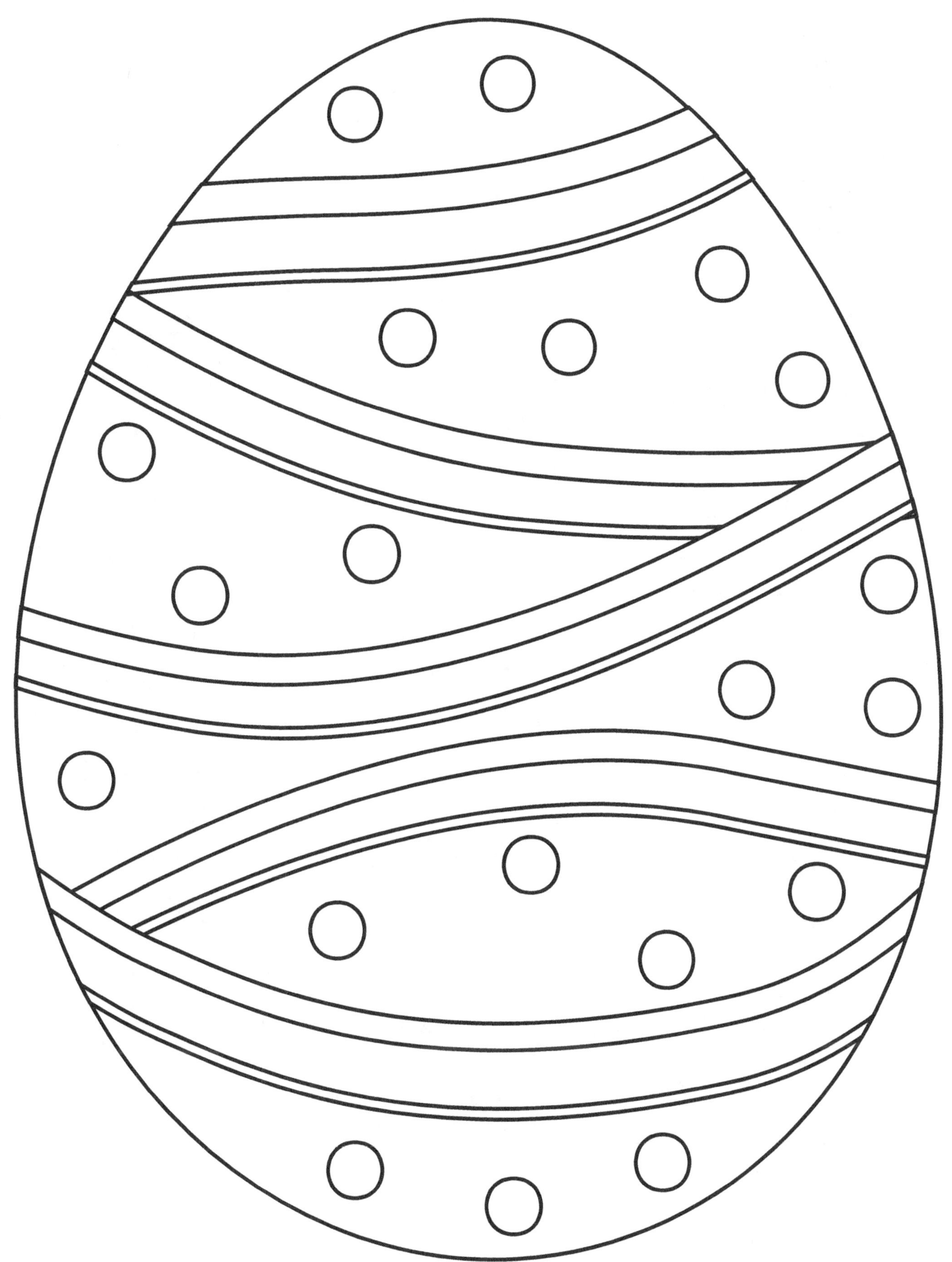

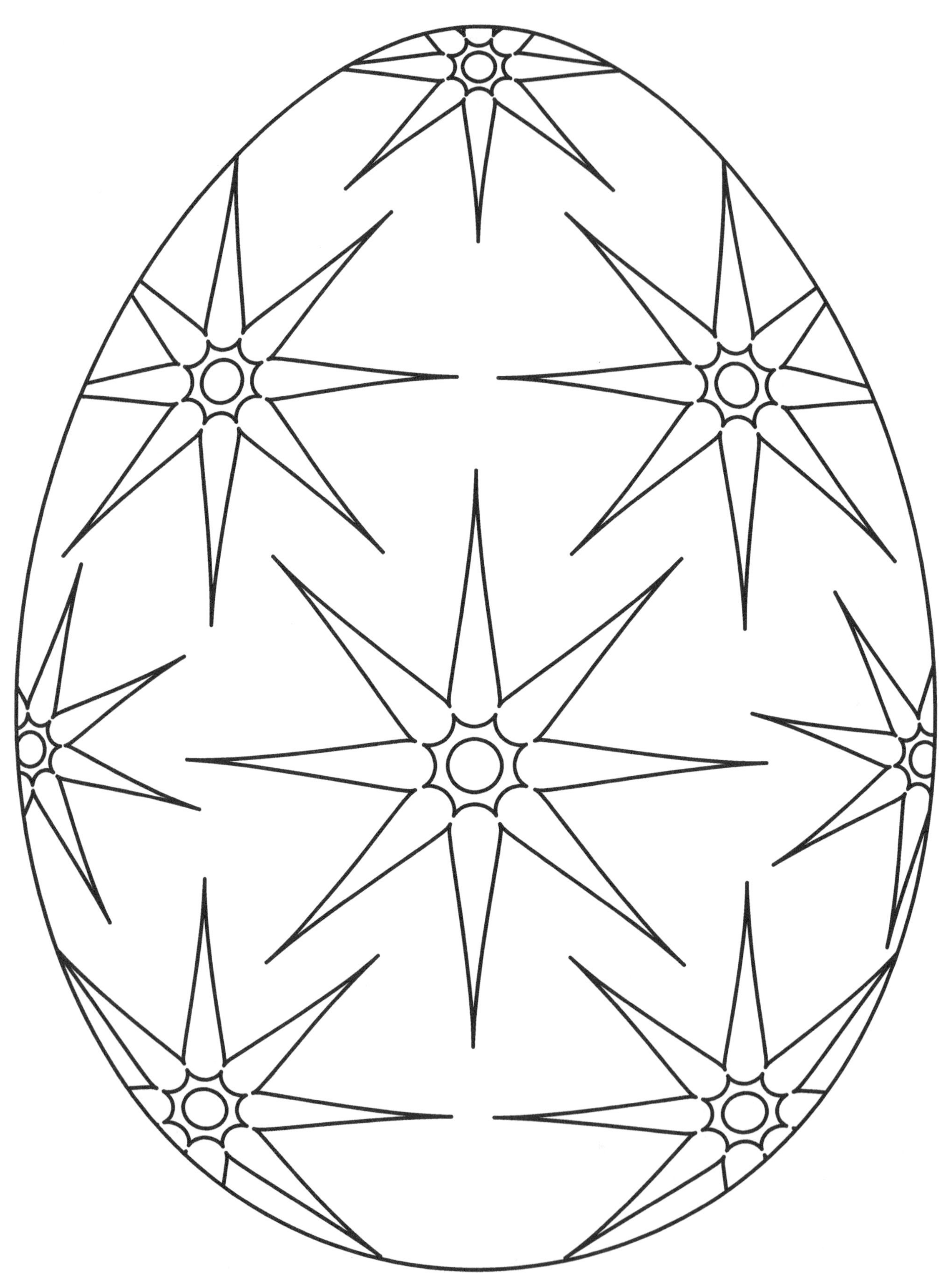

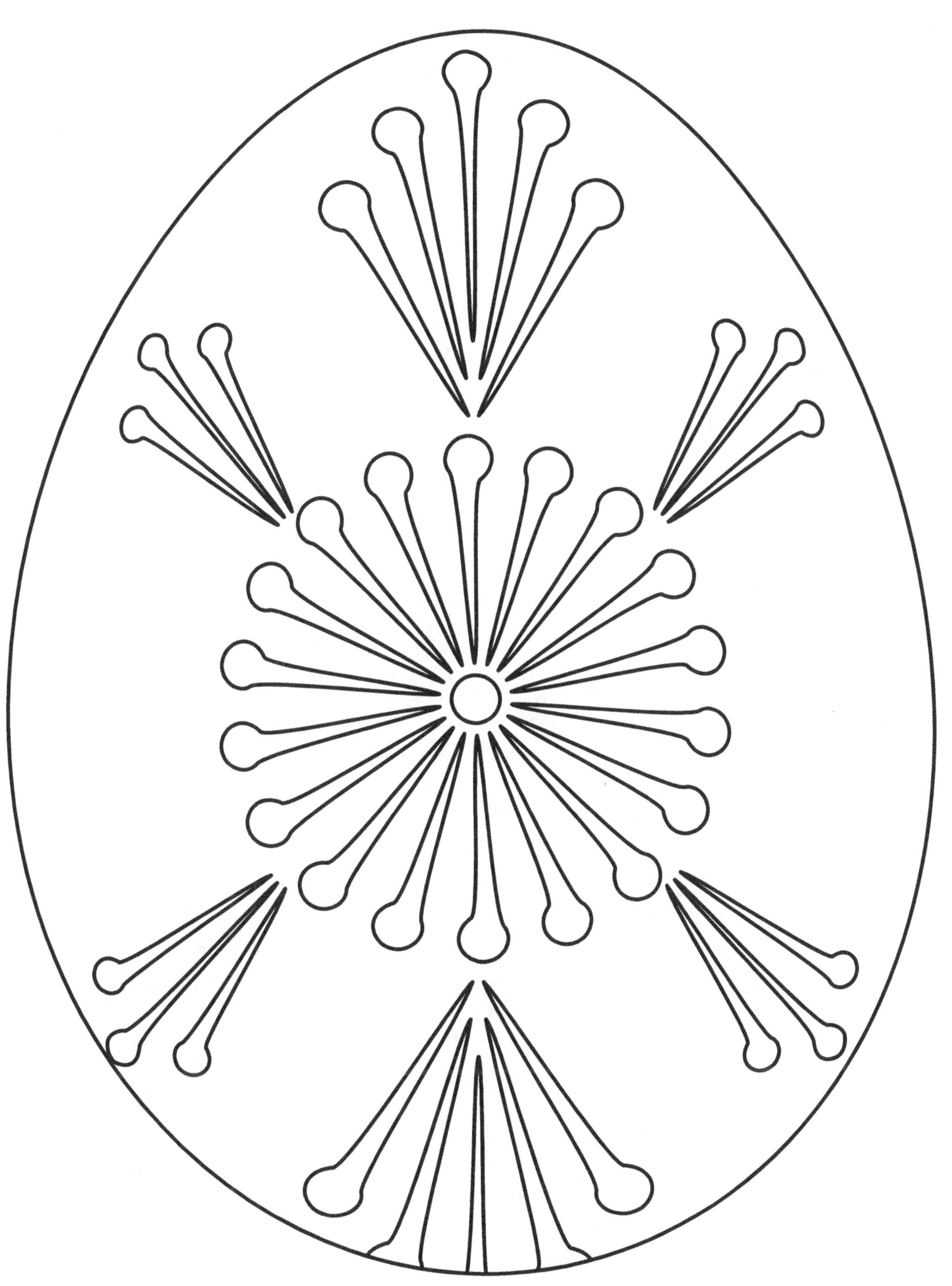

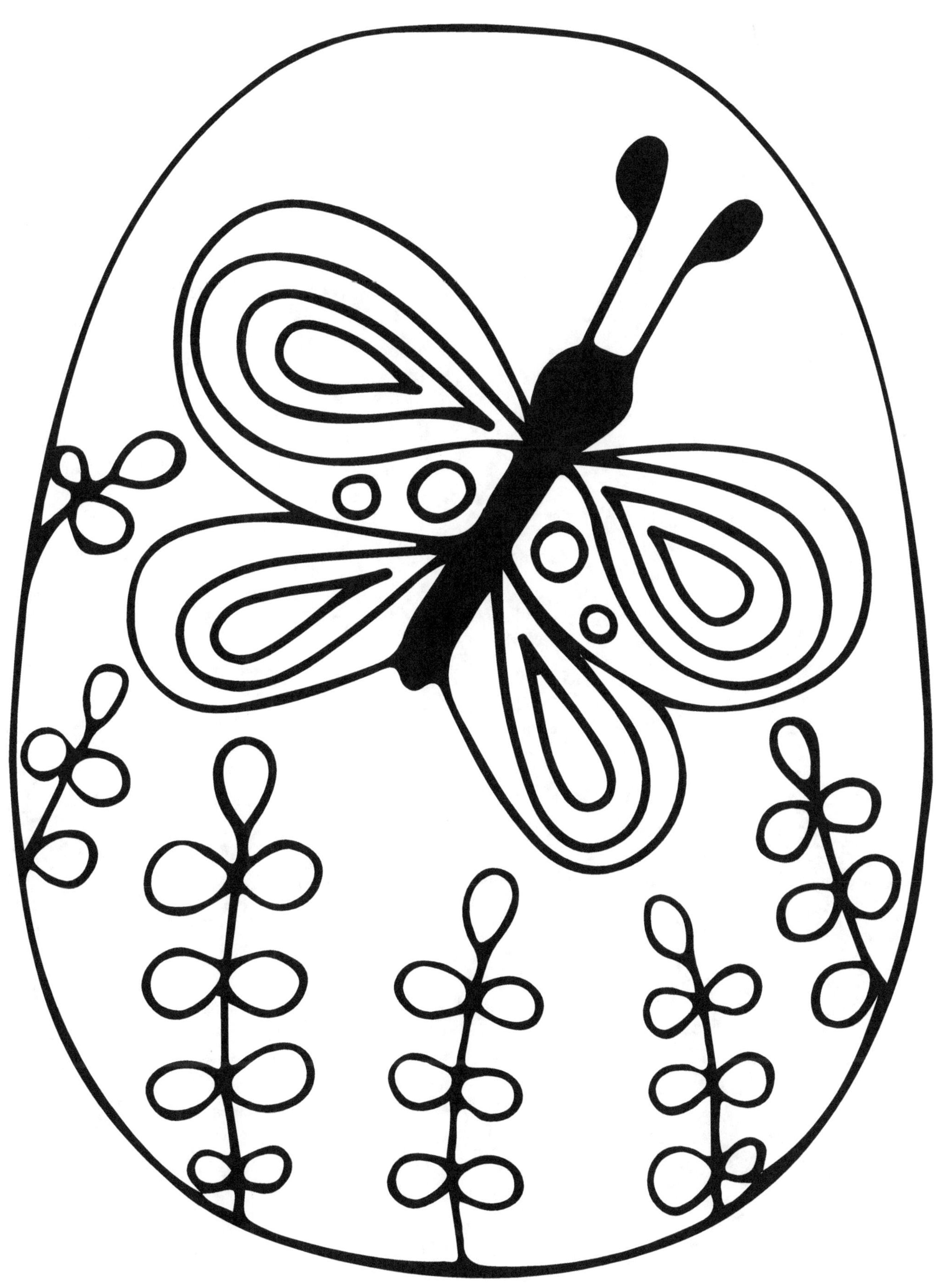

Happy Easter Coloring Book:
Eggs to Color for Family, Friends _and_ More!

Thank you for your recent purchase. We hope you've enjoyed your "Happy Easter Coloring Book" by Florabella Publishing, LLC.

Happy Easter!